Ruck 'n' Muck

GW00545365

This edition published in the UK in 2003 exclusively for

WHSmith Limited
Greenbridge Road
Swindon SN3 3LD
www.WHSmith.co.uk

Created by Essential Works
168a Camden Street
London NW1 9PT

A catalogue record for this book is available from the
British Library.

ISBN: 0 9545493 4 1

Printed and bound in Singapore

Ruck 'n' Muck

Iain Spragg

ANYONE WANT THE TROPHY?

The 1973 Five Nations Championship was a certainly a close-fought affair with all five teams winning and losing twice and the tournament ending in a unique, if highly unsatisfactory, five-way tie. So everyone shared the trophy or – to look at it another way – the wooden spoon for finishing last in the table, which takes its name from a Cambridge University tradition of awarding the college's weakest mathematician with a wooden spoon. Mind you, this was a more satisfactory outcome than in the previous year when the 1972 Championship had to be abandoned when Scotland and Wales both refused to travel to Ireland in the wake of mounting sectarian violence.

QUOTE UNQUOTE

66 South Africa were a disgrace. Corne Krige as captain targeted the entire England team. It was all rather Jurassic. 99

Sky commentator Stuart Barnes doesn't mince his words after the Springboks' record defeat at Twickenham in 2002.

SWEEPING ALL BEFORE THEM

Wales were the first team to land the Grand Slam in 1908 and repeated the feat the following season. England joined the Grand Slam club five years later, Scotland in 1925 and Ireland, for the first and to date last time, in 1948. Late entrants France recorded their first clean sweep in 1968. England hold the record for the most Grand Slams with 12. Wales have eight and the French seven. Scotland have done the clean sweep three times and Ireland once. Italy are still waiting, although they did at least make their bow in the 2000 Six Nations with a 34-20 defeat of Scotland in Rome.

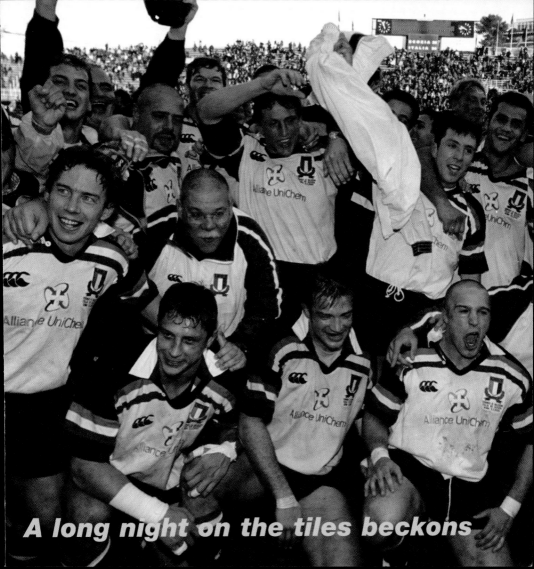

A long night on the tiles beckons

One fan who won't have to wait at the bar at half-time

TRICOLORE TRAGEDY

France may be a major force in the Six Nations these days but the Tricolores weren't always such stubborn or successful opposition. Following their debut in 1910, when the championship became the Five Nations, the French won just once in their first four seasons in the tournament when they beat Scotland by a single point in 1911. They weren't any opposition at all between 1931 and 1947 as France were thrown out of the tournament in 1931 when it emerged they were paying their players and flouting the game's strict amateur status. The Tricolores were let back in again following the end of the Second World War.

HIGH FOR LOWE

The record for the most tries scored in a championship season is jointly held by England's Cyril Lowe and Scotland's Ian Smith on eight. Lowe reached his landmark in 1914 while Smith emulated the feat 11 years later. The record for the most drop goals in a championship season is a three-way tie with five between Wales' Neil Jenkins (2001), Italy's Diego Dominguez (2000) and France's Guy Camberabero (1967). Jenkins, however, stands alone as the tournament's top scorer of all time with 406 points after making his debut against England in 1991. Prolific England fly-half Jonny Wilkinson is the championship's highest points scorer in a single game. He collected 35 points in England's 82-3 win over Italy in 2001.

'Who's stolen my flag?'

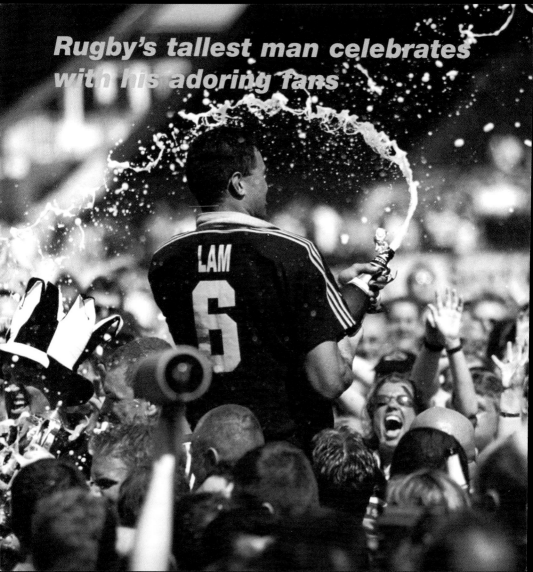

Rugby's tallest man celebrates
with his adoring fans

IN A LEAGUE OF THEIR OWN

Bath and Leicester Tigers have dominated the English league since its introduction in 1987 – claiming the title six times each. London Wasps have won the league three times with Newcastle clinching the honours just once in 1998. But Richmond hold the record for the biggest victory in English league history when they ran out 106-12 winners over Bedford in 1999. The Londoners ran in a record 16 tries in their astonishing romp, which also saw a record 13 conversions.

QUOTE UNQUOTE

66 I don't like this new law, because your first instinct when you see a man on the ground is to go down on him. 99

Sky TV commentator Murray Mexted wishes he'd kept his mouth shut. Hope his wife wasn't listening.

A BIT GAULING?

The first four European Shield finals – rugby's equivalent of football's Uefa Cup – were all-French affairs and produced four different winners. Harlequins became the first non-French finalists in 2001 and went on to break the Gallic stranglehold on the competition with 42-33 victory over Narbonne in Reading. Pontypridd became Wales' first finalists in the European Shield in 2002 but fell at the final hurdle, losing 25-22 to Sale Sharks.

Isn't it nice to be wanted?

REFRESHING SUCCESS

English clubs have claimed four Heineken Cups since its birth in 1996. France have had three champions and Ireland one when Ulster beat Colomiers in Dublin in 1999. Scottish and Italian sides are yet to claim the trophy. Toulouse won the inaugural competition in 1996 when they beat Cardiff 21-18 in a gripping match at the Arms' Park. Leicester Tigers are the only team to have successfully defended the Heineken Cup. They first won the trophy in 2001 after a 34-30 win over Stade Francais in Paris and clung on to the trophy the following season when they controversially beat Munster 15-9 in Cardiff. Munster were the defeated finalists in 2000 as well, a match which saw the lowest points total in a Heineken Cup final when Northampton edged past them 9-8 in a tense clash at Twickenham.

'Honest, I only want to shake your hand!'

FIRST INTERNATIONAL

Forty eight years after William Webb Ellis picked up the ball and ran with it at Rugby School, the traditional birth date of rugby, the sport witnessed its first international clash in 1871 between Scotland and England at Raeburn Place, Edinburgh. Both sides started with 20 players and Scotland ran out winners by a goal and a try to England's solitary goal. Ellis, having seen the sport he invented achieve Test status, died the following year.

QUOTE UNQUOTE

66 **Dusty Hare kicked 19 of the 17 points.** 99

Gaffe-prone BBC commentator David Coleman with another of his trademark classics.

THIS STONE
COMMEMORATES THE EXPLOIT OF
WILLIAM WEBB ELLIS
WHO WITH A FINE DISREGARD FOR THE RULES OF FOOTBALL
AS PLAYED IN HIS TIME
FIRST TOOK THE BALL IN HIS ARMS AND RAN WITH IT
THUS ORIGINATING THE DISTINCTIVE FEATURE OF
THE RUGBY GAME
A.D. 1823
PRESENTED BY RUGBY SCHOOL
24TH FEBRUARY 1900

A
W. WEBB ELLIS
LA F.F.R. RECONNAISSANTE
2d octobre 1960

WILLIAM WEBB ELLIS
LA
FEDERATION FRANÇAISE
DE RUGBY RECONNAISSANTE
22 OCTOBRE 1969

THE 1991 RUGBY WORLD C.U.P.
MESSAGE RELAY
TO **WILLIAM WEBB ELLIS**
WHO GAVE RUGBY
TO HIS SCHOOL IN 1823 AND
THEN TO THE WORLD

THE FIRST RUGBY PLAYER
In appreciation
THE RUGBY FOOTBALL UNION

'Taxi!'

SOUND ADVICE

Although the game had already been flourishing for over 50 years, it was not until 1883 that someone suggested referees should be equipped with whistles. Some would say they've been making up for lost time with them ever since. Or at least some have – there is not much call for whistling in International Deaf Rugby, which started in 1995 when a deaf team from South Africa toured Australia and New Zealand. South Africa won the Test series against their All Black counterparts 2-1.

KEEPING AN EYE ON THINGS

Gareth Edwards needed a police escort from the pitch after Wales' Five Nations clash with Ireland in Dublin in 1968. Even though the home side still won the match, Edwards had to be protected from the crowd after the referee awarded one of his attempted drop goals which everyone else in the crowd knew had missed by a mile. Edwards claimed the three points and the supporters went mad, claiming the referee must be blind. Well, could be – after all some players have been partially sighted, such as Scottish international Jock Wemyss who won five caps for his country after the end of World War one – despite losing an eye.

'Wanted: Boot for friendship and possible conversion'

BALLS PLEASE!

Rugby may have been created by William Webb Ellis at Rugby School in 1823 but getting hold of the right equipment in the early days was not always easy. It was left to another William, this time William Gilbert, to help the game move forward when he proudly displayed the first-ever commercially produced oval rugby ball – inflated with a pig's bladder – at the International Exhibition in London in 1851. His innovation would certainly have come in handy a few years later when a light-fingered spectator led to the abandonment of the 1877 West Wales Challenge Cup final between Cardiff and Llanelli. The 'fan' stole the ball and the game had to be called off because no-one could locate a spare!

'Hello, Mum!'

BOUNCING BACK

Beleaguered Welsh fans must have been expecting the worst again at the start of the 1993-94 season when their team suffered a humiliating 26-24 defeat against unfancied Canada. But fortunately for the supporters their team picked themselves up admirably, shrugging off their embarrassment to lift the Five Nations Trophy on points difference – their first title since 1988 – when they had shared the honours with France. To date, that remains Wales' last success in the tournament.

QUOTE UNQUOTE

66 **I think Brian Moore's gnashers are the kind you get from a DIY shop and hammer in yourself. He is the only player we have who looks like a French forward.** 99

Ex-England prop Paul Rendall waxes lyrical about his former front row colleague.

RAMPANT LIONS

England's Martin Johnson is the only man to captain the Lions twice – leading the tourists to victory in South Africa in 1997 and to an agonising 2-1 series reverse in Australia four years later. But he is not the Lions' most successful captain. That distinction belongs to Irish legend Willie John McBride, who lead the 1974 tourists to South Africa and brought them back again undefeated. McBride's tourists played 22 games, winning 21 and were only denied a 100 per cent record when the Springboks salvaged a controversial draw in the fourth and final Test.

POLITICAL DECISION

Some might say rugby and politics don't mix but that certainly wasn't the case when South Africa toured England in 1906. When the Springboks played England in the Test, the match was played in atrocious conditions and ended in a disappointing draw. The English media were upset with the result and launched a campaign to have the Test replayed, even calling in the Under Secretary of State for the Colonies at the time to give his ruling on a replay. And his name? None other than a pre-war Winston Churchill.

QUOTE UNQUOTE

66 **The convicts will smash the toffs.** 99

The ever-diplomatic David Campese makes an unconvincing attempt to calm things down ahead of another Anglo-Australian clash.

HOWZAT?

The British & Irish Lions may be rugby's most famous tourists but the side owes its very existence to cricket. During the winter of 1888, entrepreneurs Alfred Shaw and Arthur Shrewsbury, who was W.G. Grace's predecessor as England cricket captain, were managing a cricket tour in Australia when they came up with the idea of repeating the experiment with a rugby team. They approached A.E. Stoddart, a future England cricket captain himself, and a tour to the southern colonies was organised. The Rugby Football Union refused to sanction the trip but it went ahead regardless.

QUOTE UNQUOTE

66 **Blood must be freely set in motion, and the whole system continually braced to enable the brain work necessary in school, to be done. In this regard, rugby especially, is beneficial to the brain.** 99

Canon Todd, Rector of Michaelhouse School, combines biology and sport with painful results!

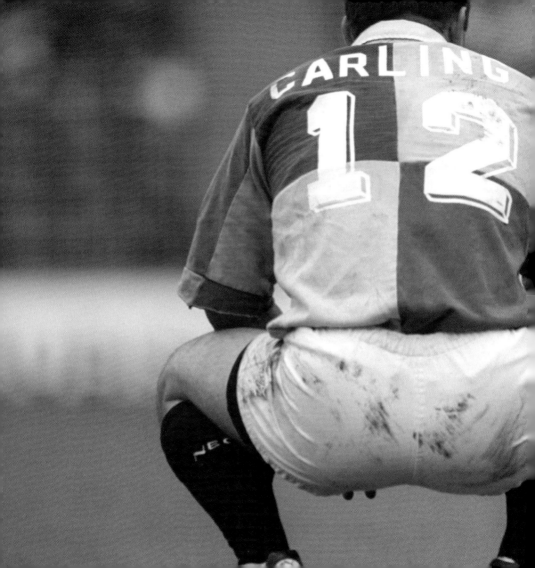

'Does my bum look big in this?'

Giant wasp strikes again!

STUNG INTO ACTION

When the Rugby Football Union was founded at a meeting in the Pall Mall restaurant in Regent Street in London in 1871, there was a notable name missing from the list of 21 original members – Wasps. No-one is quite sure why Wasps didn't make the meeting although there are two legendary theories. The first goes that the club conspired to send their representative to the wrong venue at the wrong time on the wrong day, the other version of the story was that he went to a pub of the same name and after one too many was too drunk to make it to the correct address after he realized his mistake.

WATER WORKS

No-one ever said rugby was a game for wimps, which certainly seemed to be the case according to an Australian referee ahead of the start of the 1997 Super-12 season. Asked how he would enforce a new rule outlawing the grabbing of an opponent's testicles, the quick-witted official replied: 'It is hard to detect. It depends on how much water is coming out of a player's eyes'. Former French coach Pierre Berbizier was equally cutting when he was asked about the aggressive behaviour of his players after an international. 'If you can't take a punch,' the man known as the Little General reasoned, 'you should play table tennis.'

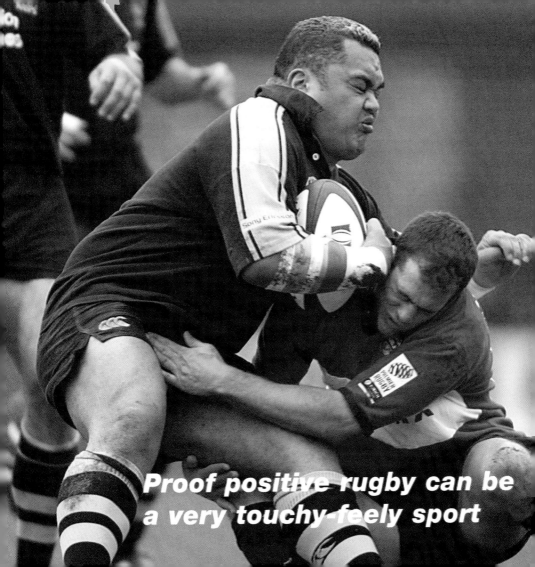

Proof positive rugby can be a very touchy-feely sport

The god of rugby makes
an unexpected appearance

NORWAY, NIL POINTS

Rugby is dominated by the Western European and big three Southern Hemisphere sides but it is also played in a surprisingly large number of countries these days. Did you know that, according to the IRB rankings for March 2003, Tunisia were ranked the 31st best side in the world? Even more surprisingly, Madagascar came in at 43rd, while the Arabian Gulf was rated 54th in the global pecking order. According to the rankings of countries affiliated to the IRB, Norway was the worst recognised rugby playing country in the world, limping in at 94th and last in the list.

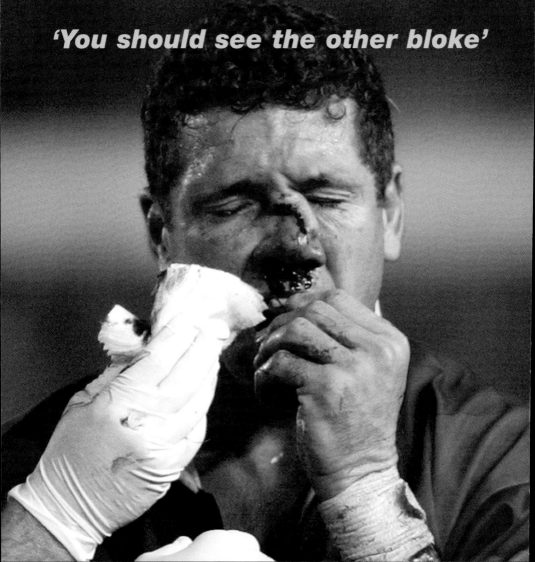
'You should see the other bloke'

A STITCH IN TIME

The mantle of the hardest man ever to play the game will be hotly disputed for decades, but All Black forward Wayne 'Buck' Shelford must surely be in with a shot after his 'heroics' in the 1986 clash with France, a match that was to later become known as the 'Battle of Nantes'. Shelford, playing only his second Test match for the Blacks, had his scrotum ripped by an errant French stud – leaving his testicle hanging out! – but ordered the New Zealand physio to stitch the wound so that he could carry on. 'I was knocked out cold, lost a few teeth and had a few stitches down below,' recalled Shelford. 'It's a game I still can't remember – I have no memory of it whatsoever.' Lucky for him!

QUOTE UNQUOTE

66 **Have a go, you mug. That means, don't die wondering whether you were good enough to win; don't wait until you've lost to see if you can win.** 99

Former Wallabies coach Bob Dwyer sums up his rugby philosophy.

THE PICKY PRESIDENT

In 1905 an appalled American President Theodore Roosevelt ordered a reform of the rules of rugby in the country after seeing photographs in a newspaper of a particularly 'bruising' game between Sarthmore and Pennsylvania. Roosevelt threatened to ban the game completely unless it was changed to please his tastes and a year later the forward pass was introduced to rugby in the States. The rules of rugby gradually died out and the game of American football, complete with padding for the more sensitive fan, was born.

Yet again the Americans take things a step too far

OLYMPIAN ACHIEVEMENT

The players in the 1908 Olympic rugby final in London between England and Australia could hardly claim tiredness as an excuse going into the match because they were actually the only two sides to enter the competition, meaning the final was in fact the first and only match of the Games, with the Wallabies claiming the gold medal and England, presumably, the silver. England's side, however, was hardly what you'd call representative of the whole country since all the players hailed from Cornwall.

QUOTE UNQUOTE

66 **It was not Hiroshima, was it?** 99

Springbok flanker Bob Skinstad calls for a sense of perspective after his Western Province side had lost to the Blue Bulls.

'I'm going home and I'm taking my ball'

USA, USA!

Believe it or not, America are the reigning Olympic rugby champions. The USA side, drawn mainly from students from Stanford University, won the title in 1924 in Paris after beating Romania and then hosts France in the final in front of a crowd of 30,000. Rugby was subsequently axed from the 1928 Amsterdam Games and the USA remain, however improbably, the Olympic champions to this day.

'Look mum, I can fly!'

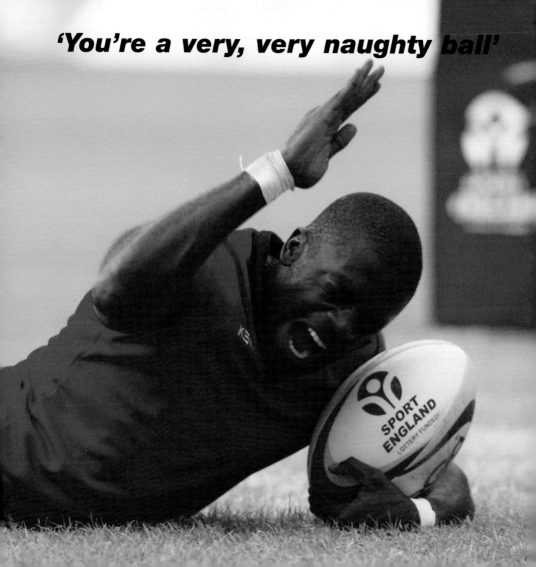

'You're a very, very naughty ball'

DYEING TO PLAY

The scheduled 1935 clash between Uganda and Kenya in Entebbe looked doomed to an early abandonment before the first whistle when both sides turned up in white shirts. Thankfully the fixture was saved when a quick-thinking female spectator produced a large bottle of black dye and proceeded to transform the Ugandan jerseys in a hastily-found iron bath tub.

Uganda has another strange rugby connection. Rugby has had many famous players but perhaps none as infamous as the young winger who was on the bench for East Africa when they entertained the 1950 British Lions. His name? None other than future Ugandan dictator Idi Amin.

Filming for the new 'Right Guard' advert gets underway

DUAL NATIONALITY

No.8 Abdel Benazzi became a French legend during his distinguished career but actually played against the Tricolores for his native Morocco in a World Cup qualifying match before switching his allegiances and making his debut for France against Australia in 1990. He is, however, far from the only rugby international to gain fame for a country other than the one of his birth. Most notable is William 'Dave' Davies who captained England 11 times from 1921 – boasting an impressive record of 10 wins and a draw – but was actually born in Wales. In terms of winning percentages, he still remains the most successful English skipper ever.

ANIMAL MAGIC

Argentina's nickname is the Pumas but it really should be the Jaguars. On their 1965 tour to South Africa, a local journalist spotted the big cat motif on the Argentinian shirts but wrongly identified it as a puma rather than a jaguar and the name, despite the howls of rugby-loving naturalists everywhere, has wrongly stuck until this day. The origin of the name 'British Lions', however, is shrouded in mystery. Adopted in the 1920s, some claim it was coined by the newspaper reporters of the time, while others argue it came from the embroidered lion motif on the ties given to the 1924 squad.

Who left the taps on?

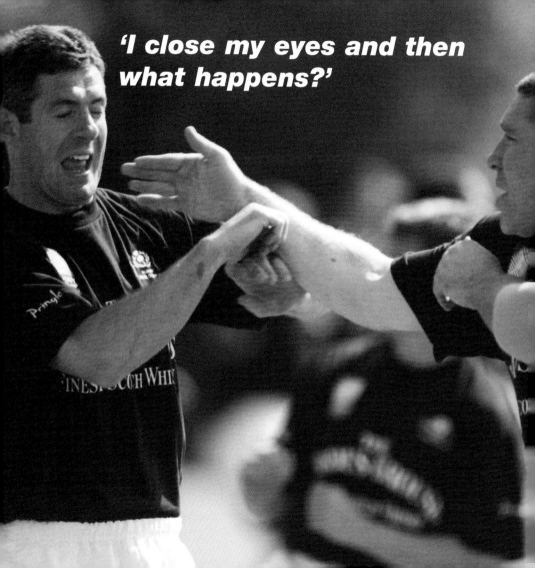

'I close my eyes and then what happens?'

NOT SO SIMPLE SIMON

All Black Simon Culhane holds the record for the most points scored in a single World Cup match after amassing 45 in New Zealand's thumping 145-17 victory over Japan in 1995 in South Africa. The previous record had been set only a week earlier by Scotland full-back Gavin Hastings, who clocked up 44 points in a comprehensive 89-0 win against the Ivory Coast. Hastings is the World Cup's highest ever points scorer and the Scotland full-back amassed 227 points after appearing at the 1987, 1991 and 1995 finals. Northampton fly-half Paul Grayson is England's top points scorer in a World Cup game – clocking up 36 points in a 1999 win over Tonga.

QUOTE UNQUOTE

66 **In September I read a lot of the (England) players' columns on websites and newspapers in which they wrote they were looking forward to the World Cup. I told them that it was one hell of a presumption to make, and that they might want to try to get a game against the All Blacks this autumn first.** 99

England coach Clive Woodward reveals his ruthless streak ahead of the 2003 World Cup.

WELSH WIZARD

Wales' Neil Jenkins is the game's highest-ever points scorer in Tests, clocking up an incredible 1049 points during his 11-year international career. He passed the mythical 1000 point barrier on Saturday, February 3 2001 against England at the Millennium Stadium. Unfortunately for Jenkins, however, Wales did not help him celebrate reaching his personal milestone in fitting fashion and lost the match 44-15. But despite his undoubted achievements, Jenkins obviously didn't always feel loved by the rugby public in the Principality. He once said: 'In Wales, the half-backs, especially the stand-off half, always get the blame.'

Neil Jenkins stoops to conquer

POLES APART

Rugby tends to polarise opinion and this is especially true of some of the men who have played the game but go on to find fame in other fields. Richard Burton, for example, said: 'Rugby is a wonderful show: dance, opera and, suddenly, the blood of a killing.' Playwright Alan Bleasdale, however, does not have such fond memories. Recalling his first game as an 11-year-old at school in Widnes, he said: 'Until I went there I hadn't even seen a rugby ball. During my first game, this huge lad came running towards me so I tripped him up – it was the only way I knew of stopping him. The PE teacher punched me in the face and the lad went on to play for England. I would have preferred to play in a more liberal environment.'

'I just want a hug'

DOUBLE CELEBRATION

The formation of the Irish Rugby Union was not exactly a triumph of administration and eventually led to a bizarre double celebration a century later. Originally 'formed' in 1874 after a meeting in Dublin, the founding members suddenly realised no-one had bothered to tell the representatives from Ulster about developments and the IRU was a member short. Five years later they had another go and 'reformed' with Ulster this time included in proceedings – which meant the IRU celebrated its centenary twice – in 1974 and 1979.

QUOTE UNQUOTE

66 **It doesn't matter how quick you are, you can't play rugby without a brain.** 99

Wallaby winger David Campese proves he's nobody's fool.

News of the free bar reaches the Ireland players

Say Cheese!

COLOUR BLIND?

Rugby has a mixed record in terms of race relations, although the early signs were very promising. The New Zealand Maori touring party in 1888, which played an incredible 74 matches in 18 months in the British Isles, actually included four white players in the squad. Predictably, however, South African rugby cannot claim to have been so open in the past and despite the SARFU being founded in 1889, it was not until 1981 in a match against Ireland that Errol Tobias became his country's first black international. The apartheid in South Africa saw the Springboks shunned by the rugby fraternity in 1984 following an England tour.

A VERY PROFESSIONAL JOB

The 1997 British & Irish Lions tour of South Africa was a watershed in the history of the game and the famous tourists. For the first time former rugby league players were selected for the Lions as coach Ian McGeechan's squad – also the first professional Lions party ever assembled – set out to tackle the Springboks. Wales' Allan Bateman, Scott Gibbs, Scott Quinnell and Dai Young, Scotland's Alan Tait and Englishman John Bentley had all swelled rugby league's ranks in the 1990s, only to return to the union fold to help the Lions to a famous 2-1 series win.

The Lions roar after dispatching the Springboks

LONG LIVE LEONARD

Jason Leonard is England's most-capped player of all time, finally notching up an amazing century of appearances for his country against France in the Six Nations in 2003. His international career, however, did not begin as promisingly on England's 1990 tour to Argentina when Leonard and his new team-mates were pelted with oranges, empty bottles and even a bath tap during a game against provincial side Tucuman. After featuring in over 100 Tests, Leonard has witnessed the game's switch to professionalism first hand. 'I can't sink 10 pints and get up and train the next morning,' he once said. 'It's a different era now.'

QUOTE UNQUOTE

66 Serious sport has nothing to do with fair play. It is bound up with hatred jealousy, boastfulness, disregard of all rules and sadistic pleasure in witnessing violence; in other words it is war minus the shooting. 99

George Orwell is clearly a big rugby fan.

Jason Leonard looks for divine inspiration

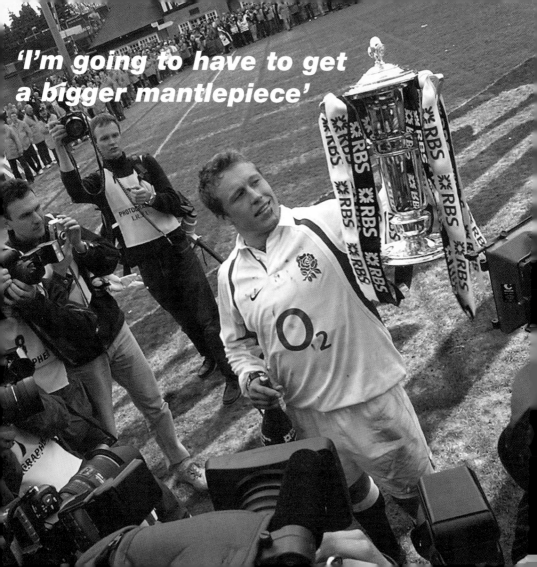

'I'm going to have to get a bigger mantlepiece'

WONDERFUL WILKINSON

Records, as the old saying almost goes, are there to be broken. Just ask Jonny Wilkinson, who has been smashing them with breathtaking speed ever since he pulled on the England shirt for the first time against the Irish in 1998. It took the young fly-half just three seasons of Test rugby to break England's previous points record of 396, which had been held by his Newcastle coach and mentor Rob Andrew, and he added to his growing collection of accolades the following year when we was awarded an MBE in the Queen's honours list – the youngest ever rugby player to be honoured in this way.

QUOTE UNQUOTE

❝ I've been watching Sven Goran Eriksson. I realise his pond is far bigger than mine, but there are similarities. ❞

Perhaps it's the goldfish! Former Wales coach Graham Henry muses on comparisons between himself and his English football counterpart.

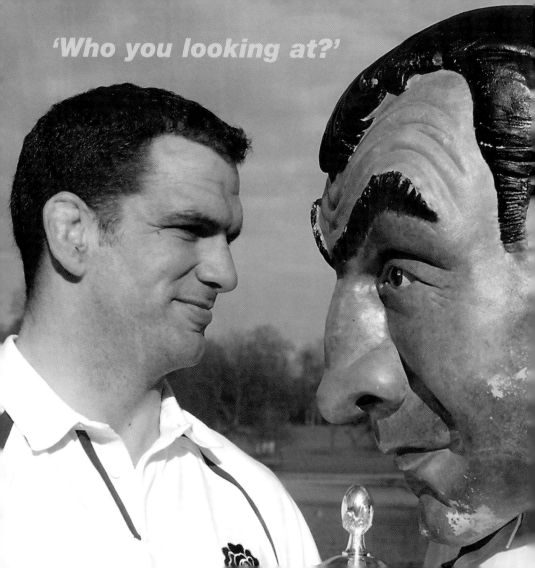

BACK WHERE HE BELONGS

Solihull-born Martin Johnson is arguably England's greatest ever captain but it could have been a very different story if the seemingly indestructible Leicester lock had not turned his back on the lure of the All Blacks. As a teenager in the late 1980s Johnson spent a year playing for King Country in New Zealand and impressed the locals so much he was selected for the All Black Under-21 side to tour Australia. Fortunately for England, the two-times Lions skipper was persuaded to come home and play for the Tigers and the rest is history. 'I haven't really read the papers,' he once said in his trademark dour drawl, 'but if they're going to call you this superhuman rugby player or whatever and you believe it, then you should also believe it when they call you a tosser.'

PITCH PARAMETERS

Rugby administrators finally realised that a dead ball line behind the try line would probably be a good idea when a Bristol player reportedly ran 300 metres beyond the goal line during an 1891 clash with Newport! Other suggested rule changes that didn't see the light of day include Lord Wakefield's idea in the 1920s to completely do away with the lineout. Wakefield wanted to adopt a football-style throw-in to any other player on the pitch but, thankfully, the powers-that-be realised they knew a bad idea when they heard one and Wakefield's idea was kicked into touch.

QUOTE UNQUOTE

66 Of all the teams in the world you don't want to lose to, England's top of the list. The English know no humility in victory or defeat. If you beat them, it's because you cheat. If they beat you, it's because they've overcome your cheating. Good teams learn how to win and lose with graciousness and humility. England hasn't learned that lesson yet. 99

Former All Black Grant Fox doesn't like the idea of losing to England.

The dangers of filling players with helium was spotted in the nick of time

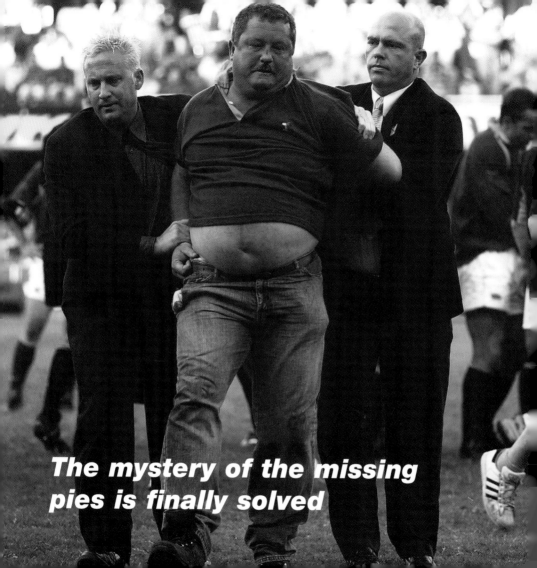

The mystery of the missing pies is finally solved

SHE'S A FEMME FATALE

During a ill-tempered clash between South Canterbury and the touring France team in 1961, one female fan was so incensed by a high tackle by Tricolores skipper Michel Crauste on one of the home players that she couldn't control herself any longer. She ran out onto the pitch to argue with Crauste, before punching him on the back of the neck with her fist to loud cheers from the home crowd.

I HAVEN'T THE FOGGIEST

The 1908 Home Nations fixture between England and Wales in Bristol was so badly affected by fog that, legend has it, Welsh full-back Bert Winfied was still out on the pitch tenminutes after the referee had blown for full time, completely oblivious to the fact everyone else had returned to the club house. Wales won the game 28-18 but only realised they were a man down when 14, rather than 15 players got in the team bath! A search party was dispatched and Winfied was finally found, peering through the fog towards where he believed his Wales team-mates were beseiging the England try line.

QUOTE UNQUOTE

"The relationship between the Welsh and the English is based on trust and understanding. They don't trust us and we don't understand them."

Former RFU supremo Dudley Wood on Anglo-Welsh relations.

ROLL OF DISHONOUR

New Zealand's Cyril Brownie earned himself the dubious distinction of becoming the first-ever player to be sent off in an international match when he was given his marching orders by referee Albert Freethy at Twickenham against England in 1925. It was to be 50 years later before England's first player – prop Mike Burton – had the bath all to himself when he was sent off against Australia. The first red cards in the Five Nations came in 1977 when Ireland's Willie Duggan and Wales' Geoff Wheel were both sent off in Cardiff. None of them, however, were in the same league as James Griffiths, who marked his Wales debut in 2000 in all the wrong ways when he was sin-binned less than 60 seconds after coming onto the pitch during a typically bruising encounter with Samoa.

'Was your card the five of clubs?'

WAS THAT THE FINAL WHISTLE?

The faint-hearted might wince at some of the modern game's physical encounters but today's matches are a picnic in comparison to the early years. Back in the 1840s, rugby was still in its infancy and judging by this article from the home of the game, Rugby School, it was an even more brutal (and long-winded) sport. According to the article: 'Hacking is permitted, but not above the knee. Holding a player carrying the ball is permitted, but with one arm only running in – the Ellis method – is permitted, but passing with the hands is banned. And if no decision is reached after five afternoons play, a match will be declared drawn.' People had to book a week off work in those days just to play!

FIRST AMONG EQUALS

Legendary All Black loose forward Michael Jones holds the distinction of being the player to score the first try in the first ever World Cup finals, held in his native New Zealand. The flanker touched down against Italy in 1987 to ensure his place in the history books. Another All Black, Samoan-born Va'aiga Tuigamala, became the first player to score a try worth five rather than four points in 1992 for New Zealand against arch-rivals Australia, after the IRB decided it wanted to encourage more open, attacking rugby.

Andre Agassi's long-lost brother is finally found

RECORD BREAKERS

Japan and Hong Kong may not be what you'd call heavyweights in world rugby but they do boast two of game's most prestigious records. Japanese winger Toru Kurihara holds the record for the most points scored in a Test match after racking up a remarkable 60 in his country's win over Chinese Taipei in a World Cup qualifier in 2003. He scored six tries and 15 conversions in Japan's slightly one-sided 152-0 victory. Hong Kong's Ashley Billington scored 50 points with ten tries against Singapore in a 1994 qualifier to set another international record.

CROWD CONFUSION

Famous Scotland international Gordon Brown became the latest in a long line of players to have the wool pulled over his eyes back in the late 60s while on tour with Glasgow District in France. Landing at the airport, Brown got off the plane to be greeted by thousands of people on the tarmac who he had been told had turned up to greet the team. Brown duly lapped up the unexpected attention, only to be told later the crowds were really there to watch Concorde making its maiden flight and not to welcome Brown and his team-mates.

QUOTE UNQUOTE

" I think you enjoy the game more if you don't know the rules. Anyway, you're on the same wavelength as the referee. "

Wales legend and BBC commentator Jonathan Davies says what everyone else has been thinking for years.

'No, I've got no idea where the rest of the team is either!'

Tuigamala – A man of many talents

SAMOAN SWITCH

International rugby has a long tradition of sides 'borrowing' players from other countries but it all got a little out of hand in the 1999 World Cup. Of the 16 sides who reached the finals, only Uruguay and Argentina drew their squads from entirely homegrown talent. The most famous international convert of the modern era is Va'aiga Tuigamala, who began his career with his native Samoa before pledging allegiance to New Zealand in 1991 in the nick of time for the World Cup finals and going on to make 19 appearances for the All Blacks.

QUOTE UNQUOTE

66 To play rugby league, you need three things: a good pass, a good tackle and a good excuse. 99

Anon.

Bill Clinton laps up the applause from his Weight Watchers group

BULKY BILL

Baseball, American Football and basketball may dominate the sporting consciousness in the United States but that didn't stop former president Bill Clinton enjoying the pleasures of rugby in his student days while he was a Rhodes Scholar studying at Oxford University. According to his contemporaries, the former president was a useful addition to their side. 'He was by no means athletic,' a former team-mate recalled. 'In fact, he was a bit lumpy but he made an excellent second row forward.' His local team in America – the Little Rock Rugby Club – have not been slow to cash in on Clinton's rugby connections, selling T-shirts boasting 'We've had Bill on our backs, now you can have him on yours.'

'I only want your shirt'

HISTORY LESSONS

Cambridge University has always laid claim to being the oldest rugby club in the world after Arthur Peel, an old boy of Rugby School, established a side in 1839. The first club to be formed outside Britain and Ireland was the Sydney University club, which was born in 1864, while the annual game between Edinburgh Academy and Merchiston Castle is the game's oldest school fixture – dating back to 1858.

QUOTE UNQUOTE

❝ If the game is run properly as a professional game, you do not need 57 old farts running rugby. ❞

Will Carling talks himself out of the England captain's job during a television interview – only to be swiftly reinstated 48 hours later following a public outcry.

ALL BLACK'S ALL WHITE

The first Test between the Lions and the All Blacks in Christchurch back in 1930 must have been a confusing affair for the assembled spectators. New Zealand actually played in white as it was felt their traditional black strip would have clashed with the Lions – who took to the field wearing dark blue. This clash of colours lead directly to the Lions adopting their now famous red shirts and New Zealand reverted back to their traditional black, much to the relief of their fans.

QUOTE UNQUOTE

❝ People back home were baying for my blood. They have got it. ❞

Under-pressure John Hart announces his retirement as New Zealand's coach after his side's shock 1999 World Cup semi-final exit to France.

Another typical night at the opera

LONG-LASTING LIONS

Modern players often complain about increasingly hectic fixture lists but they should count themselves lucky in comparison with their predecessors, such as the 1888 Lions who toured Australia and New Zealand. The team left England in early March, and returned in late November, having played a staggering 35 games en route, winning 27 and drawing six of their matches. And they did it all using just 22 players in total. The team also found time to play some Australian Rules matches against local teams while on tour, despite having no idea what the rules were!

'I can't believe they stole the toilet door'

FLYING WINGERS

The 1924 clash between England and France saw two of the most innovative, if comical tries ever to be scored at Twickenham. The first bizarre score came from England right wing Carston Catcheside who, finding himself in the clear and with only the full-back to beat a metre or so from the try line, decided to take the aerial route over his opponent and high-jumped the Frenchman and grounded the ball as he landed. The move obviously impressed the French right wing who repeated the trick in the second-half against the England full-back, conclusively proving that imitation is indeed the sincerest form of flattery.

'And now you crawl through my legs'

BRILLIANT BABAS

The world famous Barbarians were brought to life by accident rather than design when the Australian side that toured Britain in 1948 found itself short of funds to finance the long trip back home. A game between an invitational side and the Wallabies at Twickenham was quickly organised and the Barbarians were born. The side's most celebrated moment came 25 years later in Cardiff when Gareth Edwards scored what many people still believe to be the greatest try ever against New Zealand as the Barbarians ran out 23-11 winners.

QUOTE UNQUOTE

66 **I've got a personal relationship with Jesus Christ. I decided to dedicate my life to the Lord in 1993. There are a lot of things that have happened in my life that I can't explain and today was one of them.** 99

South African fly-half Jannie de Beer after he dropped a record five goals in the Springboks' win over England in the 1999 World Cup quarter-final.

Another minor dispute is amicably resolved

A FRENCH AFFRAY

Rugby is synonymous with hard men and the occasional bit of violence, although most players reserve their aggression for on the pitch. Sadly that was not the case when Brive played Pontypridd in a Heineken Cup clash in France in 1998, the result of the match completely forgotten when the two teams renewed hostilities in a local bar after the game. 'I have never seen anything so violent in my life,' said Brive fly-half Christophe Lamaison. 'It was like a Western. People were throwing doors, chairs, glasses, they were all hysterical. I even saw bottles smashed to be used as weapons.'

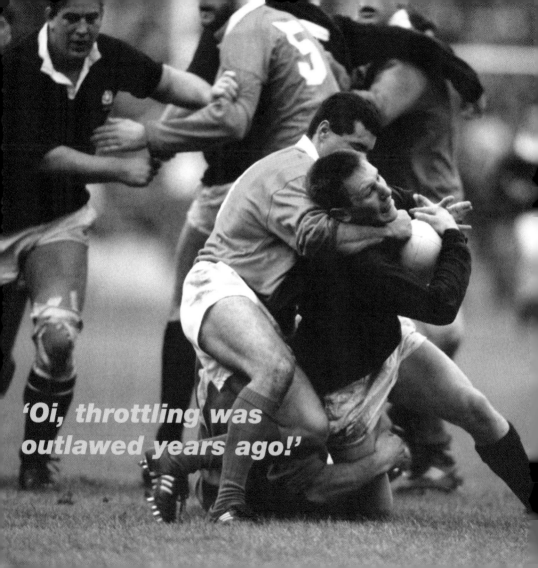

'Oi, throttling was outlawed years ago!'

RUNNING THE RULE

Rugby's rules are notoriously unfathomable to outsiders but spare a thought for the game's early pioneers, who had to put up with what seemed like constant changes to the laws of the game. For example, in 1862 Blackheath drew up its own set of rules – one of which outlawed throttling in the scrum! However, it was not until 1892 that teams were officially limited to 15 players on the pitch at any time after a ruling by the RFU. But that was nothing compared to the confusion that dogged early games in America – the first match was played in 1874 between the McGill and Harvard Universities – where, in the absence of referees, all decisions were left to the discretion of the two captains.

QUOTE UNQUOTE

66 It's like having a Ferrari in the garage and going out and catching the bus. 99

Australian centre Tim Horan gives his views after the sliding roof in the Millennium Stadium was not shut to keep out rain during the Wallabies' quarter-final clash with Wales in 1999.

SIGHT FOR SORE EYES

The first ever live radio commentary of a rugby match occurred in New Zealand back in 1926 when George Allardyce picked up the microphone and described the events during a game between Christchurch and High School Old Boys. Fans had to wait another 12 years before television got in on the act, beaming pictures of the 1938 clash between England and Scotland at Twickenham to homes in Britain and, in the process, ushering in a new era for the sport.

'Now all we need are the crowd and the players!'

PAST HIS SELLA-BY DATE?

The honour of the world's most-capped player goes to French centre Philippe Sella who played for his country a staggering 111 times. Born in 1962 on St. Valentine's Day, he was first capped twenty years later against Romania. Between 1982 and 1987 he played in a remarkable 45 consecutive games for the French. In that period he achieved two major milestones – scoring in every game of the 1986 Five Nations Championship, as well as playing in the first French team ever to beat the All Blacks the following year. He finally retired after France beat England in the third/fourth place play-off in the 1995 World Cup in South Africa.

QUOTE UNQUOTE

66 **Remember that rugby is a team game – all 14 of you make sure you pass the ball to Jonah.** 99

Rumoured fax to the All Blacks hotel the night before their 1995 World Cup semifinal demolition of England.

'Come to me,
come to me!'

DIPLOMACY, HEALEY STYLE

England winger Austin Healey is as well known for his outspoken opinions as his rugby these days, as this extract from his Guardian column during the 2001 Lions tour to Australia demonstrates; 'I was standing at the back of the press conference after the game against the Waratahs, listening to Bob Dwyer trying to squirm out of the Duncan McRae thing. I pointed to my mouth and I pointed to my backside. That stirred the Aussies up a bit.'

QUOTE UNQUOTE

66 Spin this, you Aussies: up yours. Is that enough to get into the Sydney Morning Sun Telegraph Herald Load of Shite? If ever I wanted to do something, it was beat you lot... here's to stuffing it up your so-called macho jacksie. Do you know, Justin Harrison's in the team to face us? Me and the plank. Do you think one of us will have the final say? I'll say so. 99

Healey speaks his mind again on the 2001 Lions tour.

'Everyone says this is my best side'

'I can't believe someone's left their washing line out'

SCREEN IDOL

Rugby has had many players who have also achieved great things in other sports but few can have been celebrated in an Oscar-winning film. But that was the fate of Scotland's Eric Liddell who won seven caps for his country, scoring four tries. But it wasn't Liddel's rugby talents that saw immortalised on celluloid but his gold medal in the 400 metres final at the 1924 Olympics – an achievement that was to later form the basis of the award-winning movie *Chariots of Fire*.

QUOTE UNQUOTE

66 **They have this impression of English rugby that we all play in Wellington boots and we play on grass that is two foot long.** 99

England coach Clive Woodward in the build-up to his side's famous win over the All Blacks in Wellington in 2003.

The tricolores' secret weapon:
'who are you calling chicken?'

A SLIPPERY CUSTOMER

Australia may now be known as the Wallabies but the side's first mascot was not a furry marsupial but a live snake which accompanied the squad on their 1908 tour of Britain. Unfortunately, however, their slithering companion didn't find the British climate to its liking and died hours before the team's first defeat of the tour against Llanelli. At least the snake didn't interfere with the game itself – unlike the countless cockerels, the mascot of the French national team, who are always in attendance when the Tricolores play but have yet to be taught it is poor form to strut their stuff on the pitch while the game is still going on!

PLUMBING THE GAPS

Fijian rugby is famed for its flamboyance and flair but the game on the South Sea Island probably wouldn't be what it is today without the contribution of a New Zealand plumber called Paddy Sheenan. Sheenan, who played for Otago back in New Zealand, went to Fiji in 1913 to work on the construction of a new hotel in the capital Suva and immediately saw the need to organise Fiji's disparate club system. He quickly called a meeting in his half-built hotel and the Fijian Rugby Union was born. Sheenan, perhaps unsurprisingly, was elected the first chairman and rugby in Fiji – the first recorded match was actually played in 1884 – never looked back.

The Fijians take news of their missing golf clubs badly

DISTANT COUSINS

Rugby is an increasingly global sport these days and there are few remoter outposts of the game in the world than the tiny volcanic Reunion island – a small French territory in the South Indian Ocean lying south-west of Mauritius. Despite its remoteness, the cyclones that battered the island and a population of less than 750,000, the capital St. Denis still boasts four active clubs, that play regular home and away fixtures against sides from island neighbours Mauritius and the Seychelles.

Proof positive Reunion Island has a 'small' pool of players

One scrum cap design that didn't catch on

MUSIC TO CALM THE SAVAGE BEASTS

The rugby world was shocked in 1993 when the seemingly invincible New Zealand toured the British Isles but surrendered their unbeaten record to England at Twickenham. But it was not all doom and gloom for the wounded All Blacks in the dressing room after the match when they got an impromptu visit from Kiwi pop star Neil Finn, who had been watching the game in the crowd. The lead singer of Crowded House was determined to lift his compatriots' spirits and launched into an unplugged medley of the group's greatest hits!

QUOTE UNQUOTE

66 You need a mental toughness. And probably don't need to be too bright. 99

England hooker Mark Regan explains the academic requirements for playing in the murky world of the front row.

EAR, EAR

One of the most sickening sights in rugby in recent years has to be when South Africa prop Johan Le Roux quite literally tried to take a piece out of someone during a Springboks clash with New Zealand. Le Roux was caught on camera and subsequently banned for biting All Black hooker Sean Fitzpatrick's ear but obviously felt little remorse after the incident. Quizzed about his ban, Le Roux said: 'For an 18-month suspension, I feel I probably should have torn it off. Then at least I could say, "Look, I've returned to South Africa with the guy's ear."'